Compound W...

Matching, Hidden Words and Flashcards

by C. Mahoney

Life is about choices...

Matching

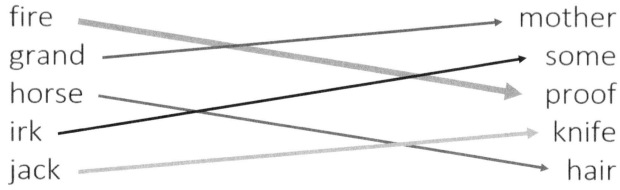

fire   mother

grand   some

horse   proof

irk   knife

jack   hair

List of Compound Words

#1: anyhow bookstore carload drawbridge eyedropper firearm grandparent housekeeper input jackhammer kinfolk limestone meanwhile newspaper offstage riverbanks saucepan tailgate uphill weatherman

#2: aircraft backtrack cardboard dishcloth everything footpath grandson honeybee iceboat jumpsuit knockdown mainstream nightfall overcharge pancake repairman supermarket toothpaste underwear waterfall

#3: aboveboard buttermilk courtroom dishwasher earthquake firefighter graveyard honeymoon ironwood jackpot kickboxing lifeboat moonscape newsletter outbreak playback raindrop soundproof underfoot waterproof

#4: airline blackjack cheesecake doorstop earthworm fireproof grandmother horsehair irksome jackknife knapsack lifeline moonshine newsprint offshoot peppermint rainfall springtime tableware uppercase

#5: afterglow bodyguard caveman dishwater earache footnote gumball housewife inmate jawbreaker kindhearted lifelong motherhood outhouse Passover racquetball superstar tailspin upload wastebasket

#6: blueprint coffeemaker driveway eyeglasses foreman grandchild however ironclad jetliner knockoff limelight moonbeam nutcracker outdo paycheck railway schoolbook thunderbird uprising waterfowl

#7: airtime background courthouse daybed eyelash firecracker grandmaster household ironwork keyhole longhorn moonstruck nearby offshore ponytail sweetheart timesaver update watchdog waterside

#8: afterlife brainwash crossword daybreak eyewitness fishhook grandmother honeysuckle icehouse lifelike moreover nothing overabundance playmate rainmaker southwest tenderfoot thunderbolt uppercut watchman

#9: airfield blueberry cheeseburger dishpan elsewhere fishbowl glassmaker hometown kettledrum mainline nevermore onward pinpoint rattlesnake someone shoelace sunglasses tenfold underground watchtower

#10: afterimage blackboard bedbug candlestick earthbound firehouse hereafter keypad newsworthy outcome overpriced playhouse somebody starfish turnover thundershower underdog undercurrent weatherproof waterwheel

#11: blacktop backstroke courtyard dogwood eyelid forearm grandfather houseboat headdress keystone newsstand overflow outline postcard seashore sideburns timekeeper underbelly upstage washtub

#12: backstage bluebird candlelight duckbill earthward footlocker granddaughter honeydew handcuff killdeer newsroom outlaw pinstripe silversmith sunfish tabletop undercut uproar wallflower wayside

#13: bookmark boardwalk caretaker cattail egghead forefather grandstand honeycomb kickstand mothball noisemaker oneself output playthings somehow sidewalk tablecloth underestimate waterway washout

#14: backspace bedclothes cabdriver earring forefinger grandma headlight housework kickback noteworthy overboard outside pacemaker raincheck supernatural Sunday typewriter upon weeknight watercolor

#15: ashtray backspin ballpark cornball forehand foothold handgun housetop keynote newsman outclass overlook subway Superman sidecar throwaway teardrop underage uproot wasteland

#16: airlift backbreaker bellbottom carryall crosscut foreclose handbook headline horseshoe highland northeast overcoat outsmart pinwheel schoolhouse skyscraper thunderstorm taillight upgrade underclothes

#17: backhand butterfingers cornmeal foreleg fishtail hammerhead headhunter killjoy nursemaid overland superscript slowdown standout teapot tailbone underachieve upriver watermelon waistband watercooler

#18: backache bluegrass backlash cargo fortnight firewater hookup horseshoe keypunch newfound outbound overweight someday sideshow taxicab turnaround underdeveloped upbeat washroom warmhearted

#19: backfire buttercup commonplace fatherland fisheye headquarters newscast overshoes outermost pinhole southwest stonewall suntan tattletale turnabout underbid upthrust whitewall weekday wartime

#20: blackbird backslide commonwealth foresee firebreak horseback housecoat oilskin outgoing sunbathe superhero stepson taxpayer timetable turnoff undercover uphold whitewash waistline watercraft

Matching Compound Words #1

Connect two words with a line to form a compound word.

any	store
book	load
car	how
draw	dropper
eye	bridge

fire	keeper
grand	parent
house	hammer
in	arm
jack	put

kin	stone
lime	stage
mean	folk
news	while
off	paper

river	man
sauce	hill
tail	pan
up	gate
weather	banks

Write each of these compound words below

_____   _____   _____

_____   _____   _____

_____   _____   _____

_____   _____   _____

_____   _____   _____

Matching Compound Words *#2*

Connect two words with a line to form a compound word.

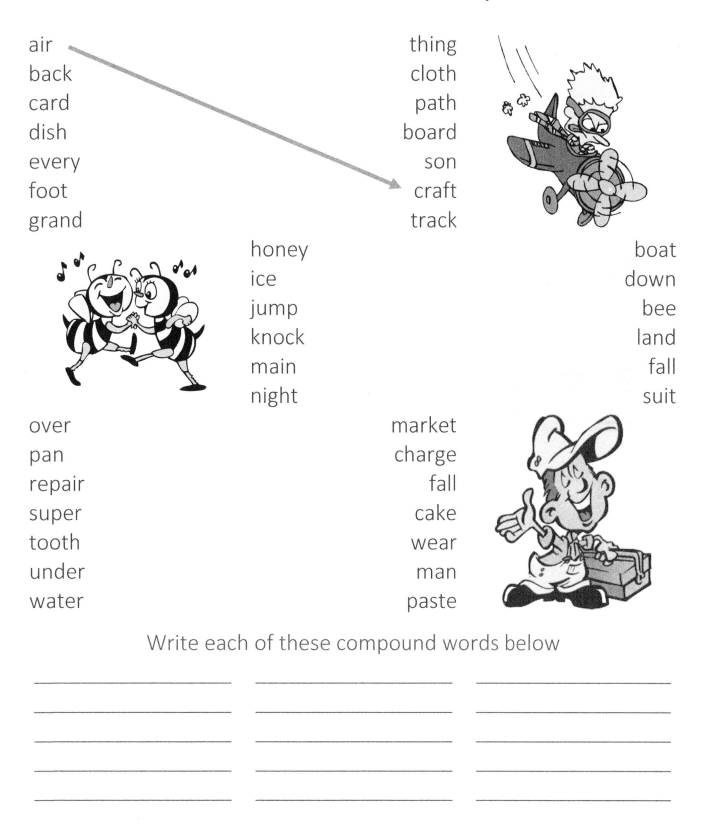

air
back
card
dish
every
foot
grand

thing
cloth
path
board
son
craft
track

honey
ice
jump
knock
main
night

boat
down
bee
land
fall
suit

over
pan
repair
super
tooth
under
water

market
charge
fall
cake
wear
man
paste

Write each of these compound words below

_____   _____   _____

_____   _____   _____

_____   _____   _____

_____   _____   _____

_____   _____   _____

Matching Compound Words #3

Connect two words with a line to form a compound word.

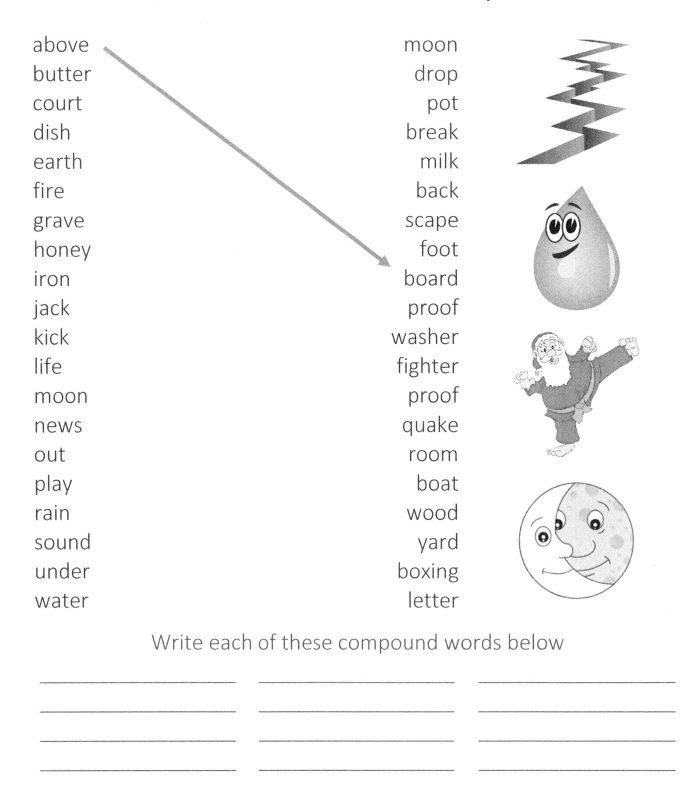

above	moon
butter	drop
court	pot
dish	break
earth	milk
fire	back
grave	scape
honey	foot
iron	board
jack	proof
kick	washer
life	fighter
moon	proof
news	quake
out	room
play	boat
rain	wood
sound	yard
under	boxing
water	letter

Write each of these compound words below

_____   _____   _____

_____   _____   _____

_____   _____   _____

_____   _____   _____

_____   _____   _____

Matching Compound Words #4

Connect two words with a line to form a compound word.

air	cake
black	worm
cheese	line
door	jack
earth	stop

fire	mother
grand	some
horse	proof
irk	knife
jack	hair

knap	shoot
life	sack
moon	sprint
new	line
off	shine

pepper	fall
rain	ware
spring	mint
table	case
upper	time

Write each of these compound words below

_____   _____   _____

_____   _____   _____

_____   _____   _____

_____   _____   _____

Matching Compound Words #5

Connect two words with a line to form a compound word.

after	guard
body	ball
cave	glow
dish	note
ear	water
foot	man
gum	ache

house	breaker
in	hearted
jaw	hood
kind	wife
life	mate
mother	long

out	load
Pass	ball
racquet	spin
super	basket
tail	house
up	over
waste	star

Write each of these compound words below

_____   _____   _____

_____   _____   _____

_____   _____   _____

_____   _____   _____

Matching Compound Words #6

Connect two words with a line to form a compound word.

blue	way
coffee	off
drive	liner
eye	light
fore	print
grand	man
how	cracker
iron	way
jet	child
knock	maker
lime	glasses
moon	rising
nut	clad
out	bird
pay	ever
rail	beam
school	fowl
thunder	do
up	check
water	book

Write each of these compound words below

_____   _____   _____

_____   _____   _____

_____   _____   _____

_____   _____   _____

_____   _____   _____

Matching Compound Words #7

Connect two words with a line to form a compound word.

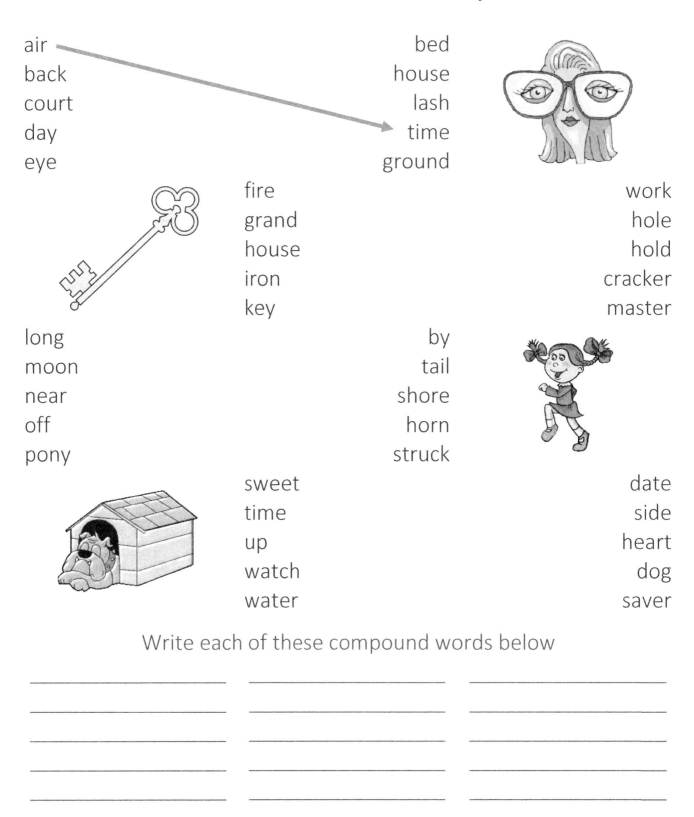

air

back

court

day

eye

bed

house

lash

time

ground

fire

grand

house

iron

key

work

hole

hold

cracker

master

long

moon

near

off

pony

by

tail

shore

horn

struck

sweet

time

up

watch

water

date

side

heart

dog

saver

Write each of these compound words below

_____   _____   _____

_____   _____   _____

_____   _____   _____

_____   _____   _____

_____   _____   _____

Matching Compound Words #8

Connect two words with a line to form a compound word.

after	witness
brain	mother
cross	hook
day	break
eye	life
fish	wash
grand	word

honey	thing
ice	abundance
life	suckle
more	like
no	house
over	over

play	west
rain	bolt
south	man
tender	mate
thunder	cut
upper	maker
watch	foot

Write each of these compound words below

_____ _____ _____

_____ _____ _____

_____ _____ _____

_____ _____ _____

_____ _____ _____

Matching Compound Words #9

Connect two words with a line to form a compound word.

air	bowl
blue	fold
cheese	lace
dish	point
else	field
fish	drum
glass	ground
home	pan
kettle	line
main	snake
never	glasses
onward	burger
pin	berry
rattle	where
some	tower
shoe	more
sun	town
ten	maker
under	one
watch	

Write each of these compound words below

_____   _____   _____

_____   _____   _____

_____   _____   _____

_____   _____   _____

Matching Compound Words #10

Connect two words with a line to form a compound word.

after	bug
black	image
bed	board
candle	bound
earth	stick

fire	after
here	come
key	worthy
news	house
out	pad

over	house
play	fish
some	over
star	priced
turn	body

thunder	current
under	wheel
under	shower
weather	dog
water	proof

Write each of these compound words below

_____   _____   _____

_____   _____   _____

_____   _____   _____

_____   _____   _____

_____   _____   _____

Matching Compound Words #11

Connect two words with a line to form a compound word.

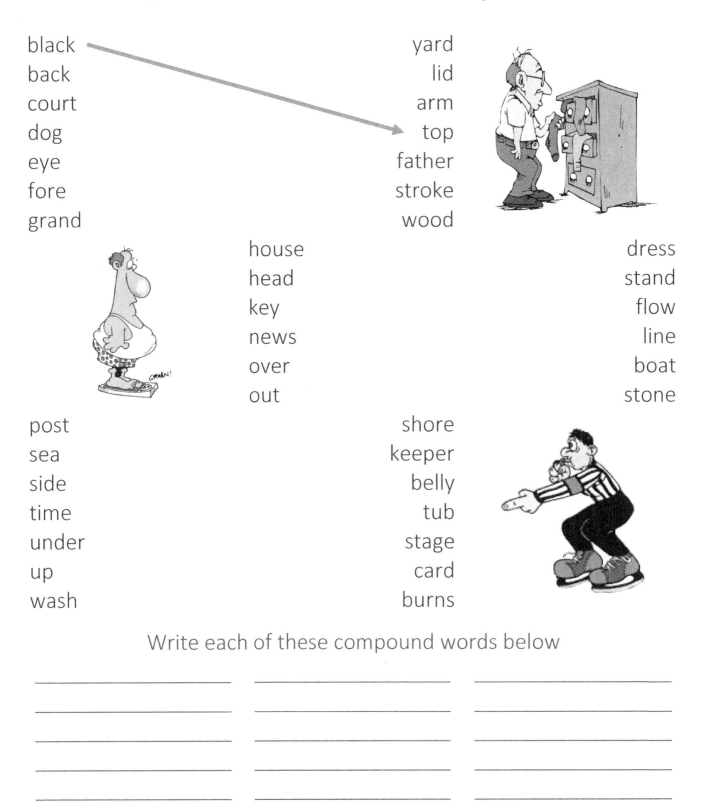

black   yard
back   lid
court   arm
dog   top
eye   father
fore   stroke
grand   wood

                    house   dress
                    head   stand
                    key   flow
                    news   line
                    over   boat
                    out   stone

post   shore
sea   keeper
side   belly
time   tub
under   stage
up   card
wash   burns

Write each of these compound words below

_____   _____   _____

_____   _____   _____

_____   _____   _____

_____   _____   _____

_____   _____   _____

Matching Compound Words #12

Connect two words with a line to form a compound word.

back	daughter
blue	locker
candle	ward
duck	side
earth	smith
foot	stage
grand	law
honey	room
hand	light
kill	bird
news	cut
out	roar
pin	bill
silver	dew
sun	flower
table	deer
under	stripe
up	fish
wall	cuff
way	top

Write each of these compound words below

_____ _____ _____

_____ _____ _____

_____ _____ _____

_____ _____ _____

_____ _____ _____

Matching Compound Words #13

Connect two words with a line to form a compound word.

book   walk
board   tail
care   mark
cat   head
egg   taker

fore   stand
grand   ball
honey   stand
kick   father
moth   comb

noise   put
one   how
out   things
play   self
some   maker

side   estimate
table   out
under   cloth
water   walk
wash   way

Write each of these compound words below

_____   _____   _____

_____   _____   _____

_____   _____   _____

_____   _____   _____

Matching Compound Words #14

Connect two words with a line to form a compound word.

back	driver
bed	ma
cab	finger
ear	light
fore	space
grand	ring
head	clothes

house		worthy
kick		board
note		side
over		work
out		maker
pace		back

rain	writer
super	night
Sun	check
type	on
up	color
week	day
water	natural

Write each of these compound words below

_____   _____   _____

_____   _____   _____

_____   _____   _____

_____   _____   _____

_____   _____   _____

Matching Compound Words *#15*

Connect two words with a line to form a compound word.

ash	top
back	gun
ball	hold
corn	tray
fore	ball
foot	note
hand	man
house	hand
key	spin
news	drop
out	park
over	away
sub	root
Super	class
side	land
throw	car
tear	look
under	way
up	age
waste	man

Write each of these compound words below

_____ _____ _____

_____ _____ _____

_____ _____ _____

_____ _____ _____

_____ _____ _____

Matching Compound Words #16

Connect two words with a line to form a compound word.

air   breaker
back   cut
bell   lift
carry   bottom
cross   all

fore   power
hand   line
head   book
horse   close
highland   shoe

north   house
over   wheel
out   east
pin   smart
school   coat

sky   light
thunder   clothes
tail   scraper
up   storm
under   grade

Write each of these compound words below

_____ _____ _____

_____ _____ _____

_____ _____ _____

_____ _____ _____

Matching Compound Words #17

Connect two words with a line to form a compound word.

back	meal
butter	hunter
corn	hand
fore	head
fish	fingers
hammer	tail
head	leg

kill	down
nurse	out
over	land
super	joy
slow	script
stand	maid

tea	melon
tail	achieve
under	cooler
up	pot
water	band
waist	bone
water	river

Write each of these compound words below

_____ _____ _____

_____ _____ _____

_____ _____ _____

_____ _____ _____

Matching Compound Words #18

Connect two words with a line to form a compound word.

back	go
blue	water
back	ache
car	bound
fort	grass
fire	found
hook	shoe
horse	lash
key	night
new	room
out	developed
over	punch
some	up
side	around
taxi	weight
turn	hearted
under	cab
up	day
wash	beat
warm	show

Write each of these compound words below

_____   _____   _____

_____   _____   _____

_____   _____   _____

_____   _____   _____

_____   _____   _____

Matching Compound Words #19

Connect two words with a line to form a compound word.

back	place
butter	eye
common	fire
father	cup
fish	land

head	most
news	hole
over	cast
outer	quarters
pin	shoes

south	tan
stone	west
sun	about
tattle	wall
turn	tale

under	day
up	time
white	bid
week	thrust
war	wall

Write each of these compound words below

_____ _____ _____

_____ _____ _____

_____ _____ _____

_____ _____ _____

_____ _____ _____

Matching Compound Words #20

Connect two words with a line to form a compound word.

back	wealth
black	break
common	back
fore	slide
fire	coat
horse	see
house	bird

oil	bathe
out	hero
sun	son
super	payer
step	skin
tax	going

time	off
turn	hold
under	wash
up	table
white	craft
waist	cover
water	line

Write each of these compound words below

_____   _____   _____

_____   _____   _____

_____   _____   _____

_____   _____   _____

_____   _____   _____

Part two

Hidden Words

List of Hidden Compound Words

#1:   anyone, airport, baseball, basketball, crosswalk, crossfire, daytime, deadline,

#2:   eyeball, eyesight, firefly, football, grandpa, grasshopper, himself, homemade,

#3:   inside, itself, jackpot, jellyfish, keyboard, kickoff, lifetime, longhouse,

#4:   moonlight, matchbox, nowhere, notebook, outfield, outfit, passport, popcorn,

#5:   quarterback, quicksand, railroad, raincoat, snowball, software, textbook, teenager,

#6:   upstream, underarm, viewpoint, viewfinder, without, whatever, yardstick, yearbook,

#7:   airplane, anything, backbone, bookshelf, carwash, comeback, daydream, daylight,

#8:   eardrum, eggshell, fireworks, footprint, goodbye, goodnight, horseplay, headache,

#9:   intake, instep, jigsaw, joystick, keyword, kneecap, lifesaver, lifeguard,

#10: moonwalk, motorcycle, newscast, nobody, oatmeal, oddball, pickup, playground,

#11: quicksilver, quickstep, rainbow, rainstorm, sidekick, softball, teacup, teamwork,

#12: upcoming, upland, voiceprint, vouchsafe, wipeout, weekend, yellowtail, yourself

#13: alongside, afternoon, anywhere, anymore, airmail, anyplace, anytime, anyway

#14: bookcase, bedroom, brainstorm, blackout, bowtie, bookworm, babysitter, blacksmith

#15: carsick, cartwheel, carpool, carefree, crossbow, carport, crewcut, clockwise

#16: forklift, forever, footrest, fireball, foothill, fisherman, forehead, forecast

#17: herself, highchair, handout, haircut, horsefly, handball, highway, handmade

#18: something, showoff, sunup, somewhere, sunflower, skateboard, sandbox, snowboard

#19: takeout, toolbox, toothpick, takeoff, teaspoon, takeover, touchdown, teammate

#20: wallpaper, warehouse, woodshop, walkway, wheelchair, wheelbarrow, washcloth, watertight

Directions

Each page has two sets of words: one that follows the theme and another that is random. Here is a sample from the first page and the explanations below:

I	R	P	A
A	Y	O	N
N	B	R	E
C	O	T	H

There are two **Compound Words**: airport, anyone

There are 33 **OTHER WORDS**: air, port, any, one, I, a, an, no, to, on, or, cot, cob, con, rot, her, pry, hen, pan, ray, bay, ban, the, yon, pray, bone, bore, core, corn, born, then, both, broth, and more. Wow! That is 33 words from just ONE of the four squares. Imagine what your students could find with perseverance and training...

What about **ABBREVIATIONS**: er (emergency room), ET (extra terrestrial), PA (Pennsylvania), CO (Colorado), NA (North America), BO (body odor), BC (British Columbia or before Christ),

What about **PROPER NOUNS**: Ron, Roy, Reno (city in Nevada), Tron (movie), Pa (short for Papa),

What about **FOREIGN WORDS**: There are none in this puzzle, but students will find them occasionally and want to know if you count them. My rule: if a word is in MY giant black dictionary, then it counts. Remember, each excluded word is a teaching moment. Enjoy!

Hidden Compound Words *#1*

Find the hidden compound words in these boxes (just like Boggle). Each letter in a word must touch the next (horizontally, vertically, or diagonally).

I	R	P	A
A	Y	O	N
N	B	R	E
C	O	T	H

	Z	I	X	
B	S	**M**	T	J
P	**O**	**S**	**S**	V
W	**I**	**B**	**L**	**E**
		N	P	R	

B	A	L	L
E	T	E	K
S	A	**B**	S
J	D	I	A

W	A	L	K
S	G	E	I
S	O	R	**C**
F	I	R	E

Y	T	I	P
A	**D**	M	E
D	E	N	T
L	I	A	S

Compound Words I found

How many compound words did you find?
5-7 Good job.   **8** = You rock!!!

Other words I found

How many other words did you find?
15-19 Good job.   **20** = You rock!!!

Hidden Compound Words #2

Find the hidden compound words in these boxes (just like Boggle). Each letter in a
word must touch the next (horizontally, vertically, or diagonally).

S	R	E	E
T	O	Y	B
H	I	E	A
G	S	L	L

F	A	T	O
A	L	B	O
Y	L	E	F
L	F	R	I

D	R	E	P
P	N	A	P
A	R	S	O
E	G	S	H

I	F	L	E
S	H	I	S
W	O	M	E
E	D	A	M

Compound Words I found
⬇

Other words I found
⬇

How many compound words did you find?
5-7 Good job.   **8** = You rock!!!

How many other words did you find?
15-19 Good job.   **20** = You rock!!!

Hidden Compound Words #3

Find the hidden compound words in these boxes (just like Boggle). Each letter in a word must touch the next (horizontally, vertically, or diagonally).

T	P	E	W
I	N	D	A
T	S	I	V
N	E	L	F

	Z	I	X	
B	S	M	T	J
P	O	S	S	V
W	I	B	L	E
	N	P	R	

O	T	L	L
P	E	O	Y
K	A	J	F
C	H	S	I

F	A	K	C
F	O	R	I
I	B	D	K
A	L	Y	E

O	I	F	E
N	L	T	I
G	O	U	M
H	U	S	E

Compound Words I found
⬇

Other words I found
⬇

How many compound words did you find?
5-7 Good job.   **8** = You rock!!!

How many other words did you find?
15-19 Good job.   **20** = You rock!!!

Hidden Compound Words #4

Find the hidden compound words in these boxes (just like Boggle). Each letter in a word must touch the next (horizontally, vertically, or diagonally).

H	B	**M**	X
C	A	O	O
T	U	R	N
H	G	I	L

	Z	I	X	
B	S	**M**	T	J
P	**O**	**S**	**S**	V
W	**I**	**B**	**L**	**E**
	N	P	R	

M	T	E	R
K	O	H	E
O	W	O	**N**
B	E	T	A

I	F	I	E
T	T	L	L
M	U	H	D
B	**O**	A	T

N	U	S	O
R	**P**	A	S
O	P	O	S
C	T	R	P

Compound Words I found

⬇

How many compound words did you find?
5-7 Good job.   **8** = You rock!!!

Other words I found

⬇

How many other words did you find?
15-19 Good job.   **20** = You rock!!!

Hidden Compound Words #5

Find the hidden compound words in these boxes (just like Boggle). Each letter in a word must touch the next (horizontally, vertically, or diagonally).

A	R	T	E
Q	U	I	R
N	D	C	B
A	S	K	A

	Z	I	X	
B	S	M	T	J
P	O	S	S	V
W	I	B	L	E
	N	P	R	

P	A	C	E
N	C	O	T
I	A	R	A
L	R	O	D

L	A	B	W
L	T	F	O
W	I	N	S
A	R	E	T

E	R	A	W
G	T	E	X
A	E	O	T
N	K	O	B

Compound Words I found
⬇

How many compound words did you find?
5-7 Good job. **8** = You rock!!!

Other words I found
⬇

How many other words did you find?
15-19 Good job. **20** = You rock!!!

Hidden Compound Words #6

Find the hidden compound words in these boxes (just like Boggle). Each letter in a word must touch the next (horizontally, vertically, or diagonally).

D	N	U	P
O	E	T	S
E	R	R	T
O	M	A	E

	Z	I	X	
B	S	M	T	J
P	O	S	S	V
W	I	B	L	E
	N	P	R	

I	F	W	E
N	D	P	I
R	E	O	V
A	T	N	I

E	V	H	O
A	T	E	U
H	I	R	T
O	W	H	A

O	O	B	R
K	Y	A	D
I	T	E	S
K	C	I	T

Compound Words I found
⬇

Other words I found
⬇

How many compound words did you find?
5-7 Good job.   **8** = You rock!!!

How many other words did you find?
15-19 Good job.   **20** = You rock!!!

Hidden Compound Words #7

Find the hidden compound words in these boxes (just like Boggle). Each letter in a word must touch the next (horizontally, vertically, or diagonally).

N	Y	H	I
A	T	G	N
I	S	E	A
R	P	L	N

	Z	I	X	
B	S	M	T	J
P	O	S	S	V
W	I	B	L	E
	N	P	R	

H	E	L	F
S	O	O	t
K	A	B	E
C	B	O	N

A	R	E	M
K	C	B	O
H	R	A	C
S	A	W	E

T	G	I	L
H	D	A	Y
E	A	R	D
B	M	A	E

Compound Words I found	Other words I found
How many compound words did you find? **5-7** Good job. **8** = You rock!!!	How many other words did you find? **15-19** Good job. **20** = You rock!!!

Hidden Compound Words *#8*

Find the hidden compound words in these boxes (just like Boggle). Each letter in a
word must touch the next (horizontally, vertically, or diagonally).

G	G	E	H
E	S	A	R
L	H	U	D
L	E	M	R

	Z	I	X	
B	S	M	T	J
P	O	S	S	V
W	I	B	L	E
		N	P	R	

O	W	T	O
R	P	E	O
K	R	I	F
S	A	N	T

Y	E	W	H
B	N	B	E
D	O	I	T
O	G	H	G

R	S	E	P
O	H	A	L
A	D	Y	K
C	H	E	C

Compound Words I found	**Other words I found**
How many compound words did you find?	How many other words did you find?
5-7 Good job. **8** = You rock!!!	**15-19** Good job. **20** = You rock!!!

Hidden Compound Words #9

Find the hidden compound words in these boxes (just like Boggle). Each letter in a word must touch the next (horizontally, vertically, or diagonally).

G	E	B	O
I	N	T	A
A	S	E	K
P	T	O	P

Z	I	X
B	S	M	T	J
P	O	S	S	V
W	I	B	L	E
N	P	R

T	I	C	E
S	O	K	A
Y	I	J	S
G	S	A	W

A	R	T	E
P	C	E	N
B	Y	E	K
W	O	R	D

R	D	O	I
A	L	I	F
R	U	G	E
E	V	A	S

Compound Words I found

How many compound words did you find?
5-7 Good job.   **8** = You rock!!!

Other words I found

How many other words did you find?
15-19 Good job.   **20** = You rock!!!

Hidden Compound Words #10

Find the hidden compound words in these boxes (just like Boggle). Each letter in a word must touch the next (horizontally, vertically, or diagonally).

L	K	M	E
A	W	O	T
E	N	O	R
L	C	Y	C

	Z	I	X	
B	S	M	T	J
P	O	S	S	V
W	I	B	L	E
	N	P	R	

Y	D	O	B
O	N	T	O
S	W	E	N
C	A	S	T

E	A	H	C
M	L	L	A
T	A	F	B
W	O	D	D

A	L	K	C
Y	P	I	U
R	G	N	P
O	U	D	A

Compound Words I found
⬇

How many compound words did you find?
5-7 Good job.   **8** = You rock!!!

Other words I found
⬇

How many other words did you find?
15-19 Good job.   **20** = You rock!!!

Hidden Compound Words #11

Find the hidden compound words in these boxes (just like Boggle). Each letter in a word must touch the next (horizontally, vertically, or diagonally).

U	I	K	S
Q	C	T	I
U	I	E	L
O	R	P	V

	Z	I	X	
B	S	M	T	J
P	O	S	S	V
W	I	B	L	E
	N	P	R	

B	O	W	L
N	S	T	O
I	A	R	R
S	F	M	A

B	T	L	I
A	L	F	O
E	D	I	S
K	I	C	K

F	R	K	L
O	T	E	A
E	W	M	C
A	R	P	U

Compound Words I found

⬇

How many compound words did you find?
5-7 Good job.   **8** = You rock!!!

Other words I found

⬇

How many other words did you find?
15-19 Good job.   **20** = You rock!!!

Hidden Compound Words #12

Find the hidden compound words in these boxes (just like Boggle). Each letter in a word must touch the next (horizontally, vertically, or diagonally).

O	C	U	L
I	M	P	A
N	O	M	N
G	A	E	D

H	S	A	F
E	C	U	E
P	I	O	V
R	I	N	T

E	N	D	L
K	E	O	U
E	I	P	T
N	W	E	S

U	R	S	F
O	E	L	L
Y	L	U	O
I	A	T	W

Compound Words I found
⬇

How many compound words did you find?
5-7 Good job.   **8** = You rock!!!

Other words I found
⬇

How many other words did you find?
15-19 Good job.   **20** = You rock!!!

Hidden Compound Words #13

Find the hidden compound words in these boxes (just like Boggle). Each letter in a word must touch the next (horizontally, vertically, or diagonally).

N	Y	P	E
A	L	T	A
N	O	I	M
G	S	D	E

	Z	I	X	
B	S	M	T	J
P	O	S	S	V
W	I	B	L	E
	N	P	R	

R	N	O	O
E	U	G	N
T	F	A	Y
E	R	O	M

E	R	E	H
C	P	Y	W
A	L	N	A
S	P	I	T

Y	N	A	P
W	A	I	R
A	B	L	M
Y	M	I	A

Compound Words I found

Other words I found

How many compound words did you find?
5-7 Good job.   **8** = You rock!!!

How many other words did you find?
15-19 Good job.   **20** = You rock!!!

Hidden Compound Words *#14*

Find the hidden compound words in these boxes (just like Boggle). Each letter in a word must touch the next (horizontally, vertically, or diagonally).

D	E	**B**	E
S	R	O	S
S	E	O	A
A	M	K	C

	Z	I	X	
B	S	**M**	T	J
P	**O**	**S**	**S**	V
W	**I**	**B**	**L**	**E**
	N	P	R	

C	H	O	R
I	T	U	I
M	K	O	**B**
S	C	A	L

N	S	T	O
I	E	O	R
A	T	W	M
R	**B**	O	O

A	O	O	K
B	**B**	T	W
Y	T	E	O
S	I	M	R

Compound Words I found
⬇

How many compound words did you find?
5-7 Good job.   **8** = You rock!!!

Other words I found
⬇

How many other words did you find?
15-19 Good job.   **20** = You rock!!!

Hidden Compound Words *#15*

Find the hidden compound words in these boxes (just like Boggle). Each letter in a word must touch the next (horizontally, vertically, or diagonally).

K	C	I	S
C	A	R	T
E	E	H	W
L	N	R	E

	Z	I	X	
B	S	M	T	J
P	O	S	S	V
W	I	B	L	E
		N	P	R	

F	E	E	R
E	R	A	D
R	A	C	S
P	O	O	L

T	F	U	R
R	O	P	A
B	O	W	C
S	S	O	R

S	A	T	U
L	C	R	C
O	W	E	W
C	K	I	S

Compound Words I found

How many compound words did you find?
5-7 Good job.   **8** = You rock!!!

Other words I found

How many other words did you find?
15-19 Good job.   **20** = You rock!!!

Hidden Compound Words *#16*

Find the hidden compound words in these boxes (just like Boggle). Each letter in a word must touch the next (horizontally, vertically, or diagonally).

A	L	**F**	T
R	I	O	F
E	Y	R	I
V	E	K	L

	Z	I	X	
B	S	**M**	T	J
P	**O**	**S**	**S**	V
W	**I**	**B**	**L**	**E**
	N	P	R	

T	B	E	R
S	A	K	I
E	L	L	**F**
R	T	O	O

R	O	L	L
E	M	A	N
H	S	O	B
I	**F**	T	O

K	E	Y	S
I	**F**	O	R
T	S	C	E
D	A	E	H

<table>
<tr><td>

Compound Words I found

⬇

</td><td>

Other words I found

⬇

</td></tr>
</table>

How many compound words did you find?
5-7 Good job.   **8** = You rock!!!

How many other words did you find?
15-19 Good job.   **20** = You rock!!!

Hidden Compound Words #17

Find the hidden compound words in these boxes (just like Boggle). Each letter in a word must touch the next (horizontally, vertically, or diagonally).

E	R	S	E
H	I	C	L
G	H	H	F
U	R	I	A

U	O	D	N
T	B	I	A
R	A	**H**	R
I	T	U	C

L	F	E	S
Y	I	O	R
A	L	L	**H**
B	D	N	A

I	G	H	W
C	**H**	A	N
B	P	D	Y
E	D	A	M

Compound Words I found

⬇

How many compound words did you find?
5-7 Good job. **8** = You rock!!!

Other words I found

⬇

How many other words did you find?
15-19 Good job. **20** = You rock!!!

Hidden Compound Words #18

Find the hidden compound words in these boxes (just like Boggle). Each letter in a word must touch the next (horizontally, vertically, or diagonally).

M	O	S	E
E	W	H	E
T	O	F	F
H	I	N	G

	Z	I	X	
B	S	M	T	J
P	O	S	S	V
W	I	B	L	E
	N	P	R	

B	E	W	O
A	R	F	L
T	N	U	S
U	P	L	A

B	O	X	W
D	L	E	H
N	O	M	E
A	S	E	R

L	O	W	O
N	S	B	A
K	E	T	R
L	A	Y	D

Compound Words I found

How many compound words did you find?
5-7 Good job.　　　**8** = You rock!!!

Other words I found

How many other words did you find?
15-19 Good job.　　　**20** = You rock!!!

Hidden Compound Words *#19*

Find the hidden compound words in these boxes (just like Boggle). Each letter in a word must touch the next (horizontally, vertically, or diagonally).

O	O	F	P
T	T	H	I
A	O	F	C
K	E	F	K

	Z	I	X	
B	S	M	T	J
P	O	S	S	V
W	I	B	L	E
	N	P	R	

P	O	O	N
S	K	A	I
A	E	T	S
O	V	E	R

X	E	O	L
I	O	B	O
T	K	A	T
E	O	U	T

A	E	U	C
M	T	O	H
M	T	E	D
A	N	W	O

Compound Words I found

⬇

How many compound words did you find?
5-7 Good job.   **8** = You rock!!!

Other words I found

⬇

How many other words did you find?
15-19 Good job.   **20** = You rock!!!

Hidden Compound Words #20

Find the hidden compound words in these boxes (just like Boggle). Each letter in a word must touch the next (horizontally, vertically, or diagonally).

U	S	W	A
O	A	E	L
H	R	B	L
E	P	A	P

A	R	R	W
B	E	E	O
L	C	H	W
H	A	I	R

S	D	Y	E
H	O	H	A
O	O	W	L
P	W	A	K

T	I	G	E
R	W	H	T
E	A	C	O
T	S	H	L

Compound Words I found

⬇

How many compound words did you find?
5-7 Good job.   **8** = You rock!!!

Other words I found

⬇

How many other words did you find?
15-19 Good job.   **20** = You rock!!!

Part three

Memory Match

Compound Words

List 1: basketball, brainstorm, crosswalk, dishwasher, driveway, eardrum, earthquake, **grasshopper**, inside, jellyfish, motorcycle, peppermint, pickup, seashore, sundown, typewriter, warehouse, weekend

List 2: airplane, carwash, comeback, courthouse, earache, eyelash, foothill, grandparent, horsefly, **ladybug**, nutcracker, playground, raincoat, soundproof, suntan, sweetheart, takeoff, turnover

List 3: coffeemaker, courtroom, forever, goodbye, handout, headache, **honeybee**, horseplay, overboard, pinhole, playhouse, postcard, raindrop, tattletale, upset, wallpaper, washtub, wastebasket

List 4: afterlife, blueberry, caveman, dishcloth, eyelid, firecracker, grandchild, headline, jellybean, overcoat, playmate, rainstorm, shoelace, **snowflake**, spacesuit, stoplight, superman, teapot

List 5: backstroke, blueprint, clockwise, doorbell, earring, eyewitness, haircut, paycheck, skyscraper, **snowman**, stopwatch, sunglasses, takeout, teardrop, teaspoon, washout, wayside, wheelchair

List 6: bookcase, cheeseburger, headquarters, herself, horseback, keyboard, meanwhile, nearby, nobody, popcorn, raincheck, **strawberry**, snowball, subway, toothpaste, touchdown, upstream, whatever

List 7: airport, anybody, baseball, cannot, **dragonfly**, firefly, grandmother, hamburger, himself, housekeeper, lifetime, moonlight, rattlesnake, sunflower, supermarket, thunderstorm, toothpick, wipeout

Each set has 36 flashcards (18 compound words).

Memory Match with Compound Words

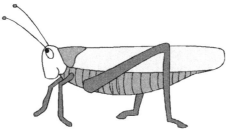

Cut these cards apart. **Mix** them up. **Turn** them upside down.
Play a game of **MEMORY** (matching two cards to form a compound word).
Take turns.   The winner is the player who has the most compound words at the end.

SET 1: grasshopper **grass**	SET 1: grasshopper **hopper**	SET 1: grasshopper **cross**
SET 1: grasshopper **walk**	SET 1: grasshopper **basket**	SET 1: grasshopper **ball**
SET 1: grasshopper **earth**	SET 1: grasshopper **quake**	SET 1: grasshopper **in**
SET 1: grasshopper **side**	SET 1: grasshopper **pepper**	SET 1: grasshopper **mint**
SET 1: grasshopper **sea**	SET 1: grasshopper **shore**	SET 1: grasshopper **dish**

SET 1: grasshopper	SET 1: grasshopper	SET 1: grasshopper
washer	**pick**	**up**
SET 1: grasshopper	SET 1: grasshopper	SET 1: grasshopper
week	**end**	**brain**
SET 1: grasshopper	SET 1: grasshopper	SET 1: grasshopper
storm	**ware**	**house**
SET 1: grasshopper	SET 1: grasshopper	SET 1: grasshopper
sun	**down**	**jelly**
SET 1: grasshopper	SET 1: grasshopper	SET 1: grasshopper
fish	**type**	**writer**
SET 1: grasshopper	SET 1: grasshopper	SET 1: grasshopper
ear	**drum**	**drive**
SET 1: grasshopper	SET 1: grasshopper	SET 1: grasshopper
way	**motor**	**cycle**

Memory Match with Compound Words

Cut these cards apart. Mix them up. Turn them upside down.
Play a game of MEMORY (matching two cards to form a compound word).
Take turns. The winner is the player who has the most compound words at the end.

SET 2: ladybug	SET 2: ladybug	SET 2: ladybug
lady	bug	car
SET 2: ladybug	SET 2: ladybug	SET 2: ladybug
wash	come	back
SET 2: ladybug	SET 2: ladybug	SET 2: ladybug
eye	lash	grand
SET 2: ladybug	SET 2: ladybug	SET 2: ladybug
parent	nut	cracker
SET 2: ladybug	SET 2: ladybug	SET 2: ladybug
horse	fly	play

SET 2: ladybug	SET 2: ladybug	SET 2: ladybug
ground	rain	coat
SET 2: ladybug	SET 2: ladybug	SET 2: ladybug
sound	proof	sun
SET 2: ladybug	SET 2: ladybug	SET 2: ladybug
tan	take	off
SET 2: ladybug	SET 2: ladybug	SET 2: ladybug
air	plane	turn
SET 2: ladybug	SET 2: ladybug	SET 2: ladybug
over	ear	ache
SET 2: ladybug	SET 2: ladybug	SET 2: ladybug
foot	hill	sweet
SET 2: ladybug	SET 2: ladybug	SET 2: ladybug
heart	court	house

Memory Match with Compound Words

B-e-e

Cut these cards apart. **Mix** them up. **Turn** them upside down.
Play a game of **MEMORY** (matching two cards to form a compound word).
Take turns. The winner is the player who has the most compound words at the end.

SET 3: honeybee **honey**	SET 3: honeybee **bee**	SET 3: honeybee **coffee**
SET 3: honeybee **maker**	SET 3: honeybee **court**	SET 3: honeybee **room**
SET 3: honeybee **for**	SET 3: honeybee **ever**	SET 3: honeybee **good**
SET 3: honeybee **bye**	SET 3: honeybee **hand**	SET 3: honeybee **out**
SET 3: honeybee **head**	SET 3: honeybee **ache**	SET 3: honeybee **horse**

SET 3: honeybee	SET 3: honeybee	SET 3: honeybee
play	over	board
SET 3: honeybee	SET 3: honeybee	SET 3: honeybee
pin	hole	play
SET 3: honeybee	SET 3: honeybee	SET 3: honeybee
house	post	card
SET 3: honeybee	SET 3: honeybee	SET 3: honeybee
rain	drop	tattle
SET 3: honeybee	SET 3: honeybee	SET 3: honeybee
tale	up	set
SET 3: honeybee	SET 3: honeybee	SET 3: honeybee
wall	paper	wash
SET 3: honeybee	SET 3: honeybee	SET 3: honeybee
tub	waste	basket

Memory Match with **Compound Words**

Cut these cards apart. __Mix__ them up. __Turn__ them upside down.
__Play__ a game of **MEMORY** (matching two cards to form a compound word).
Take turns. The winner is the player who has the most compound words at the end.

SET 4: snowflake **snow**	SET 4: snowflake **flake**	SET 4: snowflake **after**
SET 4: snowflake **life**	SET 4: snowflake **blue**	SET 4: snowflake **berry**
SET 4: snowflake **cave**	SET 4: snowflake **man**	SET 4: snowflake **dish**
SET 4: snowflake **cloth**	SET 4: snowflake **eye**	SET 4: snowflake **lid**
SET 4: snowflake **fire**	SET 4: snowflake **cracker**	SET 4: snowflake **grand**

SET 4: snowflake	SET 4: snowflake	SET 4: snowflake
child	head	line
SET 4: snowflake	SET 4: snowflake	SET 4: snowflake
jelly	bean	over
SET 4: snowflake	SET 4: snowflake	SET 4: snowflake
coat	play	mate
SET 4: snowflake	SET 4: snowflake	SET 4: snowflake
rain	storm	shoe
SET 4: snowflake	SET 4: snowflake	SET 4: snowflake
lace	space	suit
SET 4: snowflake	SET 4: snowflake	SET 4: snowflake
stop	light	super
SET 4: snowflake	SET 4: snowflake	SET 4: snowflake
man	tea	pot

Memory Match with Compound Words

__Cut__ these cards apart. __Mix__ them up. __Turn__ them upside down.
__Play__ a game of **MEMORY** (matching two cards to form a compound word).
Take turns. The winner is the player who has the most compound words at the end.

SET 5: snowman	SET 5: snowman	SET 5: snowman
snow	man	back
SET 5: snowman	SET 5: snowman	SET 5: snowman
stroke	blue	print
SET 5: snowman	SET 5: snowman	SET 5: snowman
clock	wise	door
SET 5: snowman	SET 5: snowman	SET 5: snowman
bell	ear	ring
SET 5: snowman	SET 5: snowman	SET 5: snowman
eye	witness	hair

SET 5: snowman	SET 5: snowman	SET 5: snowman
cut	pay	check
sky	scraper	stop
watch	sun	glasses
take	out	tear
drop	tea	spoon
wash	out	way
side	wheel	chair

Memory Match with Compound Words

Cut these cards apart. Mix them up. Turn them upside down.
Play a game of MEMORY (matching two cards to form a compound word).
Take turns. The winner is the player who has the most compound words at the end.

SET 6: strawberry **straw**	SET 6: strawberry **berry**	SET 6: strawberry **book**
SET 6: strawberry **case**	SET 6: strawberry **cheese**	SET 6: strawberry **burger**
SET 6: strawberry **head**	SET 6: strawberry **quarters**	SET 6: strawberry **her**
SET 6: strawberry **self**	SET 6: strawberry **horse**	SET 6: strawberry **back**
SET 6: strawberry **key**	SET 6: strawberry **board**	SET 6: strawberry **mean**

page 2 (cut apart)

SET 6: strawberry	SET 6: strawberry	SET 6: strawberry
while	**near**	**by**
no	**body**	**pop**
corn	**rain**	**check**
snow	**ball**	**sub**
way	**tooth**	**paste**
touch	**down**	**up**
stream	**what**	**ever**

Memory Match with Compound Words

Cut these cards apart. **Mix** them up. **Turn** them upside down.
Play a game of **MEMORY** (matching two cards to form a compound word).
Take turns. The winner is the player who has the most compound words at the end.

SET 7: dragonfly **dragon**	SET 7: dragonfly **fly**	SET 7: dragonfly **air**
SET 7: dragonfly **port**	SET 7: dragonfly **any**	SET 7: dragonfly **body**
SET 7: dragonfly **base**	SET 7: dragonfly **ball**	SET 7: dragonfly **can**
SET 7: dragonfly **not**	SET 7: dragonfly **fire**	SET 7: dragonfly **fly**
SET 7: dragonfly **grand**	SET 7: dragonfly **mother**	SET 7: dragonfly **ham**

SET 7: dragonfly	SET 7: dragonfly	SET 7: dragonfly
burger	**him**	**self**
SET 7: dragonfly	SET 7: dragonfly	SET 7: dragonfly
house	**keeper**	**life**
SET 7: dragonfly	SET 7: dragonfly	SET 7: dragonfly
time	**moon**	**light**
SET 7: dragonfly	SET 7: dragonfly	SET 7: dragonfly
rattle	**snake**	**sun**
SET 7: dragonfly	SET 7: dragonfly	SET 7: dragonfly
flower	**super**	**market**
SET 7: dragonfly	SET 7: dragonfly	SET 7: dragonfly
thunder	**storm**	**tooth**
SET 7: dragonfly	SET 7: dragonfly	SET 7: dragonfly
pick	**wipe**	**out**

Printed in Great Britain
by Amazon

43615961R00037